THE UKULELE

SOLOING
SECRETS BOOK FOR BEGINNERS

TERRY CARTER

UKELIKETHEPROS

ISBN-13: 9781735969220
Copyright 2021
TERRY CARTER
UKELIKETHEPROS.COM
Designed by: M. @itsmariway

TABLE OF CONTENTS

THE ESSENTIALS

It is important to learn and memorize these terms and symbols because they not only apply to ukulele but to all music.

Treble Clef or "G" Clef

Staff

Time Signature

Bar Line

End

Measure Numbers

Measure or Bar

Top Number:
How Many Beats Per Measure

♩ = 120 ○— **Tempo Marks**
120 bpm (beats per minute)

Repeat Sign

Bottom Number:
What Kind of Note Gets the Beat

Common Time:
Same as 4/4 Time

Notes On The Staff: There are seven notes in music (A, B, C, D, E, F, G) and they move up and down alphabetically on the staff.

G A B C D E F G A B C D E F G A B C D E F

How To Remember The Notes:

Notes On The Lines

Notes in The Spaces

E (every)   G (good)   B (boy)   D (does)   F (fine)   F   A   C   E

HOW TO READ TAB

Tablature (TAB) is a form of music reading for ukulele that uses a 4 line staff and numbers. Each line of the staff represents a string on the ukulele and the numbers represent which fret you play on. When looking at the TAB staff it reads like it's upside down on the paper compared to the strings of your ukulele. On the TAB staff, the highest line (closest to the sky) represents the 1st string (A string) of the ukulele, while the lowest line (closest to the ground) represents the 4th string (G string) of the ukulele. When you see 2 or more notes stacked on top of each other on the TABB staff, that means you play those notes at the same time, like a a chord.

UKULELE STRINGS

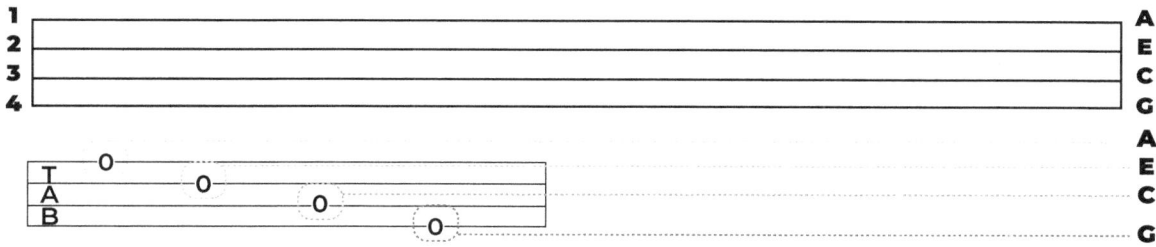

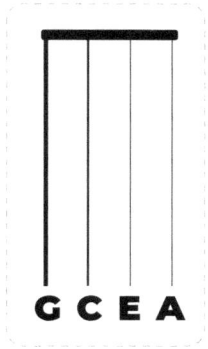

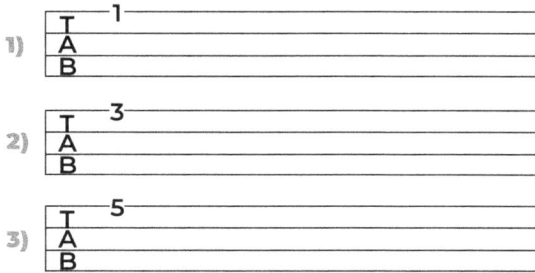

1rst STRING EXAMPLES

1) A string. FIRST FRET.
2) A string. THIRD FRET.
3) A string. FIFTH FRET.

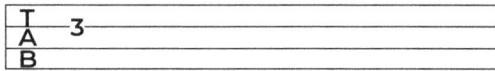

2nd STRING - E string. THIRD FRET.

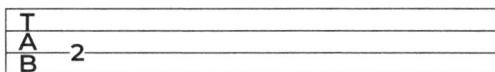

3rd STRING - C string. SECOND FRET.

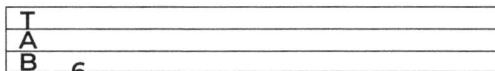

4th STRING - G string. SIXTH FRET.

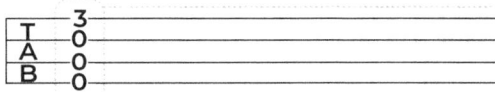

CHORD C

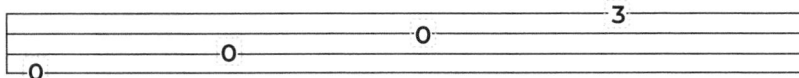

ARPEGGIO
USING THE C CHORD

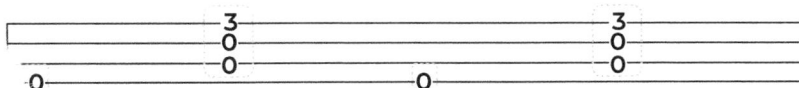

PINCH
USING THE C CHORD

WHAT THE STUDENTS SAY:

"For scores of ukulele players like myself who are not great singers, I was elated by the way in which fingerpicking techniques gave voice to my music.

And those electrifying riffs that set my soul on fire? I now have the means to let rip and play them! Whether you are a novice or seasoned ukulele player, fingerpicking is the ideal way to expand your musical repertoire. Take note:

This is your opportunity to break loose from the chords that bind you!"

MALCOLM KLEIN
UKULELE STUDENT.

THE UKULELE

SOLOING
SECRETS BOOK FOR BEGINNERS

Welcome to the Ukulele Soloing Secrets Book For Beginners! Learning how to solo is one of the biggest mysteries that ukulele players face. It is also one of the most requested topics that I get at ukelikethepros.com. So here you go: a book to answer all the questions you may have about how to solo on the ukulele. All the lessons for this book are written for ukuleles tuned G-C-E-A, and will only use strings 1-3, so it doesn't
matter if you have High G or Low G ukulele.

For this book we are going to start at the very beginning. That means you do not need to have any prior experience soloing to take this book. I am going to walk you step-by-step through the process that I use to solo; the same process that has helped me to be a successful musician for over 30 years.

When it comes right down to it, soloing is not that hard if you understand the process and have the necessary foundation of knowledge and technique required to be a great soloist. I'm going to teach you this knowledge and show you these techniques.

I have broken the Ukulele Soloing Secrets Book For Beginners down into three sections. Each section will focus on learning how to play and use one scale. These three scales, the Major Scale, The Blues Scale, and the Major Pentatonic Scale, are the most widely used

and important scales that you need to know. If you can learn and memorize these three scales, you are on your way to being able to solo over all styles of music.

Once you learn these three scales, you need to know how to apply them to soloing over a chord progression. In each section I took a popular chord progression that fits perfectly over these scales. Although the chord progressions are not the focus of the book, it is important to understand the key and the chords that you are soloing over.

In section one, where we learn the Major Scale, we are going to use the simple chord progression that you hear on songs like "Brown Eyed Girl," a simple I-IV-I-V progression. Don't worry if you don't understand what I-IV-I-V means, it's simply the C-F-C-G chords. I have taken this chord progression and written a solo for you using the Major Scale. This first solo that you will learn is melodic and smooth-sounding, and will start to give you the ability to take the Major Scale and make it musical.

In section two, we focus on the Blues. Not only will we play over a standard 12-bar Blues progression in the key of C, but we will also use the Blues Scale. The Blues is the most important style of music you can learn, as it has influenced virtually every genre of music. Plus, the Blues scale is one of the coolest sounding scales that you will learn. It sounds great over tons of different musical styles. For this section, the Blues solo I have written for you focuses more on learning common licks and phrases that will help you sound like a pro in no time. The cool thing is that once you learn these licks, you will be able to apply them while soloing over your favorite songs.

In section three, we take it to the backroads with the Major Pentatonic Scale and a Johnny Cash-style chord progression. Although the Major Pentato nic scale isn't as well known as the Blues or the Major Scale, it is absolutely vital if you love Country, Americana, Folk, Rock, and Christian music. The solo that I wrote for you here will weave between two different patterns of the Major Pentato-

nic scale, and will show you some of the hottest country licks you have ever heard.

Don't forget this is all designed for the beginner, and I promise you this will unlock the mysterious world of soloing. But, we are not done!

The last step in your journey to being a great soloist is to learn how to do it yourself. That's right, you need get your hands dirty in order to have the confidence to solo like you know you can. In the last lesson for each section, I'm going to show you how to write your own solos using the Major Scale, the Blues Scale, and the Major Pentatonic Scale. These will be the most important lessons in this book because I'm going to teach exactly how to combine the scale and the licks that I show you to create your own solo that will knock your socks off.

Sound Good?

Well, it's time. There is nothing more I can say that will help you become a great soloist. It's now your turn to dive into the *Ukulele Soloing Secrets Book for Beginners.*

C MAJOR SCALE

In this section we are going to explore the C Major Scale. The Major Scales are by far the most widely used scales when creating melodies and solos in literally all genres of music, including rock, pop, folk, jazz, gospel, and country. The C Major Scale is a great place to start because the notes of the scale are C-D-E-F-G-A-B-C, which as you can see contains no sharps (#) or flats (b). The Solfege method of teaching music (Do-Re-Mi-Fa-Sol-La-Ti-Do) is also based off the Major Scale. Get this scale memorized and get the notes in your hands and your ear and it will help guide you to creating great solos.

This section of the Major Scale is broken into 3 parts:

Part One: You will learn how to play the one-octave C Major Scale both ascending and descending strings 1-3 on your ukulele. Octave just means you're playing the scale from one C note to the next highest-sounding C note.

C Major Scale

Part Two: You will learn how to play a melodic solo using the C Major Scale. This solo only uses the notes of the C Major Scale, but adds various rhythms and phrases to make it sound like a solo. By learning this solo you will start to develop the skills that are necessary to play and write great sounding solos. You will learn this solo over the C-F-C-G7 chord progression which can be heard on many songs including "Brown Eyed Girl" by Van Morrison.

Part Three: Action time.
In this section you will write your very own solo. By taking what you learned in parts 1 and 2, you will craft a solo that fits your style and vibe. This is the time to be creative and let your talents shine. As long as you play the notes from the C Major Scale, your solo will sound great over the C-F-C-G7 chord progression.

You can also get free access to the backing tracks at:
UKELIKETHEPROS.COM/SOLOBOOK

C MAJOR SCALE

The Major scale is an extremely important scale to know and memorize. It is used to create melodies and licks in every style of music including rock, pop, folk, chrisitan, classical, country, and jazz. Make sure to get this open position version down so you can play it without looking at your music. You may also recognize this scale as
SOLFEGE: Do Re Mi Fa Sol La Ti Do.
You can play this on any ukulele tuned G-C-E-A, with high or low g.

♩=100

ULTP PACKS
TERRYCARTERMUSICSTORE.COM

WHAT THE STUDENTS SAY:

"The "Soloing" Zoom/Youtube classes are really
good. Very engaging for all levels;
easy to access for the very beginner,
and also enlightening for folks like me who are
beginning the ukulele but are longtime guitar
players who have been less-than-confident
in our soloing skills.

I approach my ukulele learning with 'new eyes',
and with no claim that my past guitar playing
-beyond the fact that I'm pretty good at finger
picking- means that I can't always learn
things from basic lessons. I always do.

In fact, I have found that embracing a
'let's just start from the beginning' view is great.
I gained a fair bit of confidence from these
sessions, even though I've played guitar
for more than 30 years".

"An open mind can bring gifts."

JIM SATOLA
UKULELE STUDENT.

C MAJOR SCALE *SOLO*

This lesson will use the C Major scale in a melodic and rhythmic way to create a solo that is smooth and sounds great. The chord progression used for this solo is a simple I - IV - I - V or C - F - C - G in the key of C. Use the same fingerings that you use when you play the Major scale for this solo. Work on getting this solo and these licks memorized so you can use them later when you create your own solos. You can play this on any ukulele tuned G-C-E-A high or low g. You can use your thumb to play the entire solo.

Pop Rock

♩=96

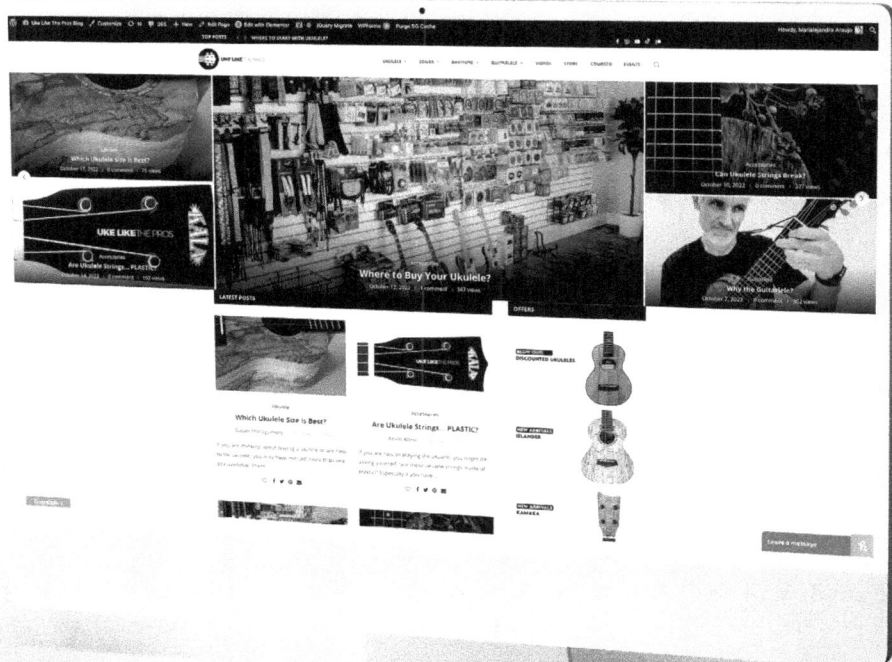

WRITE YOUR OWN *SOLO*
C MAJOR SCALE

Use the C Major scale to write your own solo. Don't be intimidated with this, it is all part of the process of becoming a great soloist. Here are 5 tips to help you write a solo: (1) Start off by playing the C Major scale up and down using quarter notes. (2) Play the C Major scale but alter the rhythm using half, quarter and eighth notes (3) Use the C Major scale but only play on 2 strings only, either strings 1 and 2 or strings 2 and 3 (4) Start with the solo you learned from the last lesson but add some variation (i.e. change the rhythm or repeat certain notes) (5) Add articulations such as vibrato, slides, hammer-ons, pull-offs, and bends. You can use your thumb to play the entire solo.

Pop Rock
♩=96

C	F	C	G7

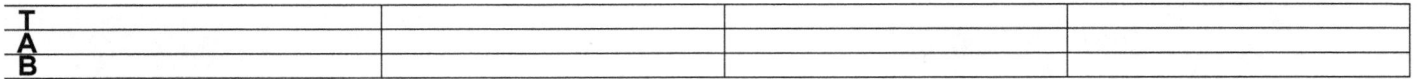

Counting: 1 + 2 + 3 + 4 +   1 + 2 + 3 + 4 +   1 + 2 + 3 + 4 +   1 + 2 + 3 + 4 +

C	F	C	G7

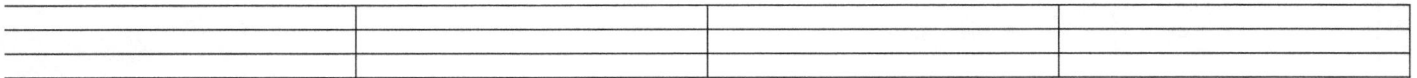

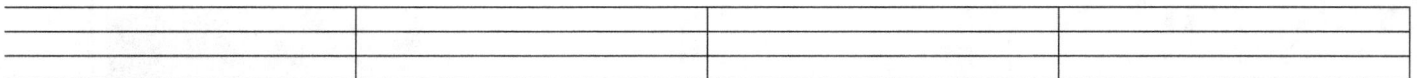

1 + 2 + 3 + 4 +   1 + 2 + 3 + 4 +   1 + 2 + 3 + 4 +   1 + 2 + 3 + 4 +

C	F	C	G7

1 + 2 + 3 + 4 +   1 + 2 + 3 + 4 +   1 + 2 + 3 + 4 +   1 + 2 + 3 + 4 +

C	F	C	G7	C

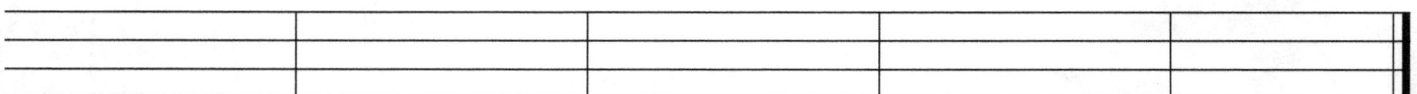

1 + 2 + 3 + 4 +   1 + 2 + 3 + 4 +   1 + 2 + 3 + 4 +   1 + 2 + 3 + 4 +   1   2   3   4

BLUES SCALE

In this section we are going to get down with the C Blues Scale. The Blues Scale is almost identical to the Minor Pentatonic Scale, but the Blues Scale adds the "Blue Note." The C Minor Pentatonic Scale is a 5-note scale: C-Eb-F-G-Bb, while the C Blues Scale is C-Eb-F-Gb-G-Bb. The Gb note, also known as the Flat 5 in the C Blues Scale really gives it that deep soulful Blues sound.

You can use the Blues Scale to solo over almost every style of music, and it really shines in the Blues, Rock, Reggae, Fusion, and Christian styles of music. You can also hear the Blues Scale with such artists as Jimi Hendrix, Muddy Waters, Stevie Ray Vaughan, Eric Clapton, T-Bone Walker, and Jimmy Page.

Although the Blues Scale has more of a minor sound, it has been used by so many different genres of music that our ears have adapted to it sounding good on almost anything. If you can learn the Blues Scale, it will help you sound great in all your soloing situations.

This section of the Blues Scale is broken into three parts:

Part One: You will learn how to play the one octave C Blues Scale both ascending and descending strings 1-3 on your ukulele. Octave just means you're playing the scale from one C note to the next highest-sounding C note.

C Blues Scale

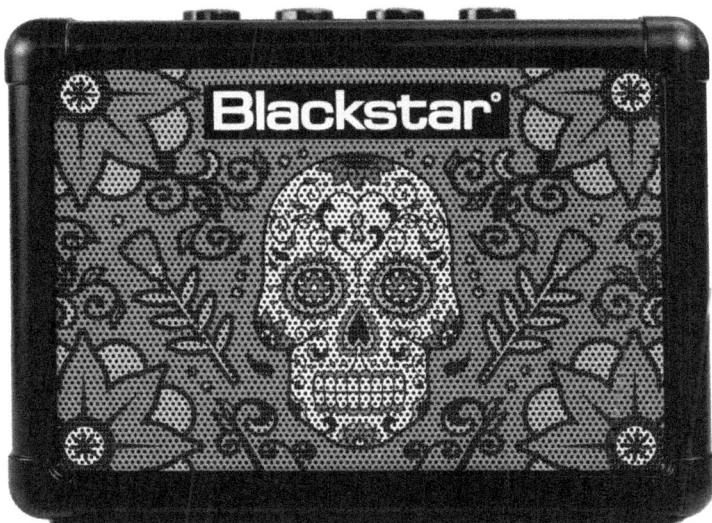

Part Two: You will learn how to play a down home, backroad Blues solo. This solo uses licks and ideas that are commonplace in the Blues world, and will help you sound like a real Blues ukulele player. This solo will be played over a traditional 12-bar Blues progression played in the swing or shuffle feel.

12 Bar Blues Form in C

Part Three: In this section you will write your very own Blues solo. You can use any notes of the Blues scale, any licks from the Blues solo, or come up with your own ideas to create a solo that burns. Any notes of the C Blues Scale will work over any of the chords in the 12-bar Blues, so let your imagination go wild as you create your solo.

(See page 17 to start writing your own solos)

Become a **PLATINUM MEMBER** and get access to:

- More Than 20 **Online Courses.**
- Weekly **LIVE Q&As.**
- Monthly **Challenges And Giveaways.**
- Be Part Of The **ULTP NATION**, The Best Ukulele Community.

BLUES SCALE

The Blues scale is one of the most widely used scales for all styles of music. The Blues scale is used regularly when soloing in blues, rock, funk, and jazz. It is very important to memor ze this scale using the proper fingerings. You can play this on any ukulele tuned G-C-E-A high or low g.

BLUES SCALE SOLO
PG. 1 of 2

This lesson will use the C Blues scale in a super cool way to create a solo that sounds bluesy and authentic. The chord progression is a traditional 12 bar Blues in the key of C using the I - IV - V or C 7- F7 - G7 chords. The licks and ideas you learn in this solo come right from the Blues scale and can be used in any Blues song, or song in the key of C where you want a Blues sound. Work on getting this solo and these licks memorized so you can use them later when you create your own solos. You can play this on any ukulele tuned G-C-E-A high or low g. You can use your thumb to play the entire solo.

Join us for our community events at **UKELIKETHEPROS.COM/JOIN**

WRITE YOUR OWN *SOLO*
BLUES SCALE

Use the C Blues scale to write your own solo. Don't be intimidated with this, it is all part of the process of becoming a great soloist. Here are 5 tips to help you write a solo: (1) Start off by playing the C Blues scale up and down using quarter notes. (2) Play the C Blues scale but alter the rhythm using half, quarter and eighth notes (3) Use the C Blues scale but only play on 2 strings only, either strings 1 and 2 or strings 2 and 3 (4) Start with the solo you learned from the last lesson but add some variation (i.e. change the rhythm or repeat certain notes) (5) Add articulations such as vibrato, slides, hammer-ons, pull-offs, and bends. You can use your thumb to play the entire solo.

Blues Shuffle

♩=100

C7

```
T
A
B
```

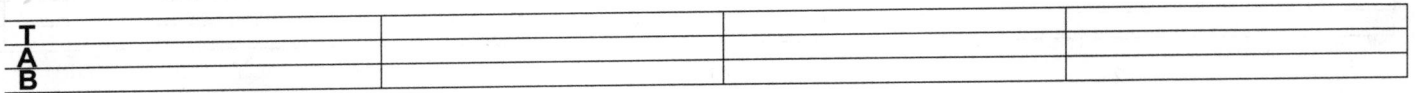

Counting: 1 + 2 + 3 + 4 +   1 + 2 + 3 + 4 +   1 + 2 + 3 + 4 +   1 + 2 + 3 + 4 +

F7   C7

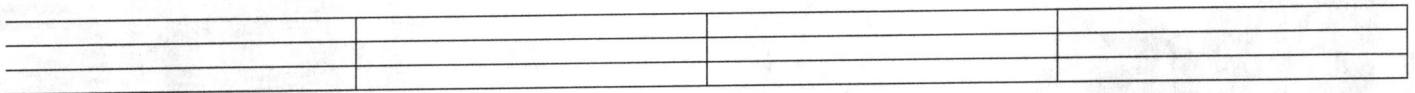

1 + 2 + 3 + 4 +   1 + 2 + 3 + 4 +   1 + 2 + 3 + 4 +   1 + 2 + 3 + 4 +

G7   F7   C7   G7   C7

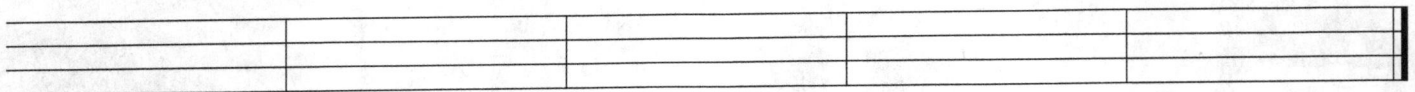

1 + 2 + 3 + 4 +   1 + 2 + 3 + 4 +   1 + 2 + 3 + 4 +   1 + 2 + 3 + 4 +   1 + 2 + 3 + 4 +

You can post your progress and see how others are doing at the UKELIKETHEPROS.COM Forum.

MAJOR PENTATONIC SCALE IN 'C'

In this section we are going to learn how to play hot licks using the C Major Pentatonic Scale. Although this scale works great over classic country tunes by artists like Johnny Cash and Buck Owens, it is also used in rock and blues by players such as Eric Clapton and Jimi Hendrix. The C Major Pentatonic Scale is similar to the C Major Scale minus 2 notes. The 5 notes of the Major Pentatonic are C-D-E-G-A, while the C Major Scale is C-D-E-F-G-A-B-C. The omission of the F and B notes in the C Major Pentatonic Scale may not seem like much, but if used correctly it can give you a unique and amazing sound for Country, Rock, Folk, Americana, Pop, and Blues styles of music.

This section of the Major Pentatonic Scale is broken into three parts:

Part One: You will learn two different variations of the C Major Pentatonic Scale. The first variation uses open strings to give you a nice lush and twangy sound. The second variation will move you up the neck and get you ready to play cool articulations like hammer-ons and pull-offs.

C Major Pentatonic Scale #1

C Major Pentatonic Scale #2

Part Two: You will learn how to play a "hot" country solo using both variations of the C Major Pentatonic Scale. This solo will use open string licks, bends, hammer-ons, and pull-offs to get your fingers boot scootin' across the fretboard. You will play this solo over a Johnny Cash style country track that uses the C-F-G7 chords.

Part Three: In this section you will write your very own Country solo using the Major Pentatonic Scale. You can use any notes for either or both of the Major Pentatonic Scales, any licks from the Country solo, or come up with your own ideas to create a "hot" country solo. Any notes from either C Major Pentatonic Scale will work over any of the C-F-G7 chord progression, although your ear will tell you that certain notes sound better over certain chords. Trust your ear and your instincts and have fun.

MAJOR PENTATONIC SCALE IN 'C'

The Major Pentatonic scale works great in country, rock, and Christian styles. It is very close to the Major scale except it leaves out the F and the B notes. You will learn two variations of the Major Pentatonic scale as they both lend themselves to different licks when playing a solo. As with all your scales, it's important to get these memorized.
You can play this on any ukulele tuned G-C-E-A high or low g.

♩=100

C Major Pentatonic Scale #1

Fingering: 2   3   3   3   2

```
T |-----------0----3----|-0----3----0--------|-----------0---------|
A |-0----2--------------|-------------3------|-0-------2-----0-----|
B |---------------------|--------------------|---------------------|
```

♩=100

C Major Pentatonic Scale #2

Fingering: 1   3   1   3   1   3   1   3   1   3   1

```
   |---------------------|----3--5--3---------|--------------------|
   |-------------3-------|-5------------------|-5--3---------------|
   |-0--2--4------------|--------------------|--------4--2--0-----|
```

You can also get free access to the backing tracks at:
UKELIKETHEPROS.COM/SOLOBOOK

This lesson will use the C Major Pentatonic scale in a hot country solo. This solo is based off two variations of the Major Pentatonic scale. Each variation of the scale provides cool and unqiue licks that can be played over a chord progression in the key of C. The chord progression used for this solo is a simple I - IV - V or C - F - G chords. Work on getting this solo and licks memorized so you can use them later when you create your own solos. You can play this on any ukulele tuned G-C-E-A high or low g.
You can use your thumb to play the entire solo.

Country Shuffle

♩=110

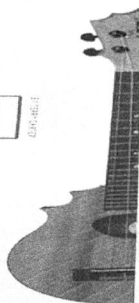

WRITE YOUR OWN *SOLO*
MAJOR PENTATONIC SCALE IN 'C'

Use the Major Pentatonic scale to write your own solo. Don't be intimidated with this, it is all part of the process of becoming a great soloist. Here are 5 tips to help you write a solo: (1) Start off by playing the Major Pentatonic scale up and down using quarter notes. (2) Play the Major Pentatonic scale but alter the rhythm using half, quarter and eighth notes (3) Use the Major Pentatonic scale but only play on 2 strings only, either strings 1 and 2 or strings 2 and 3 (4) Start with the solo you learned from the last lesson but add some variation (i.e. change the rhythm or repeat certain notes) (5) Add articulations such as vibrato, slides, hammer-ons, pull-offs, and bends. You can use your thumb to play the entire solo.

Country

♩=110

C

```
T
A
B
```

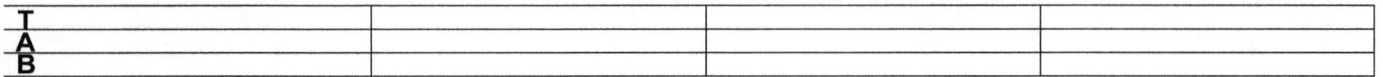

Counting: 1 + 2 + 3 + 4 +   1 + 2 + 3 + 4 +   1 + 2 + 3 + 4 +   1 + 2 + 3 + 4 +

F

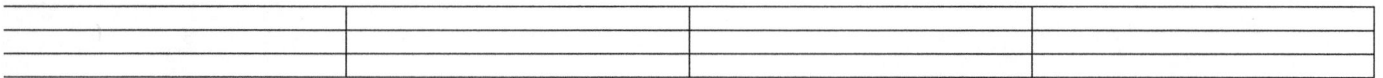

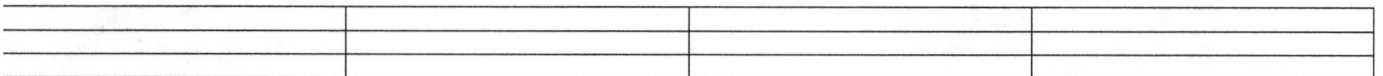

1 + 2 + 3 + 4 +   1 + 2 + 3 + 4 +   1 + 2 + 3 + 4 +   1 + 2 + 3 + 4 +

G

1 + 2 + 3 + 4 +   1 + 2 + 3 + 4 +   1 + 2 + 3 + 4 +   1 + 2 + 3 + 4 +

C   F   C   G   C

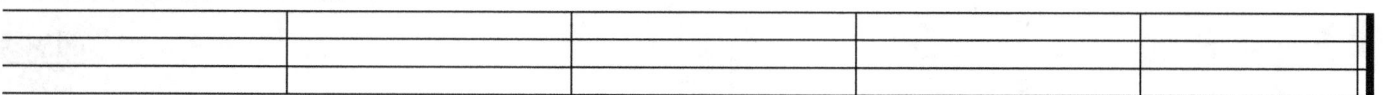

1 + 2 + 3 + 4 +   1 + 2 + 3 + 4 +   1 + 2 + 3 + 4 +   1 + 2 + 3 + 4 +   1 2 3 4

BONUS
MATERIAL

Expand your knowledge with four more
essential scales that you need to know to help
you improve your soloing techniques.

Let's do this!

NATURAL MINOR SCALE *in C*

The Natural Minor scale is Godfather of minor scales and helps derive the other minor scales such as the Minor Pentatonic, Harmonic Minor, and Melodic Minor scales. The Natural Minor scale takes the Major Scale and flats the 3rd, 6th, and 7th degrees of the scale giving you C - D - Eb - F - G - Ab - Bb - C.

♩=100

C Natural Minor Scale

Fingering: 2 3 1 3 4 1 3 1 4 3 1 3 2

You can post your progress and see how others are doing at the **UKELIKETHEPROS.COM** Forum.

MINOR PENTATONIC SCALE *in C*

The Minor Pentatonic is a 5-note scale that is like the little brother to the Blues scale. The Minor Pentatonic scale is essentially the same as the Blues scale, but the Blues Scale adds one extra note (the b5 or Gb note). The solo in this book uses the Blues scale, but if you can play the Blues Scale you can play the Minor Pentatonic scale.

♩=100

C Minor Pentatonic Scale

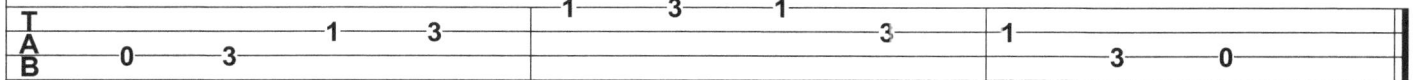

HARMONIC MINOR SCALE *in C*

The Harmonic Minor scale is a unique scale that invokes mystical sounds of the middle-east. This scale gets its sound by the 1 1/2 step interval between the Ab and the B notes. This scale can be heard in styles such as rock, jazz, metal and neo-classical music. This scale will add a cool new sound to your soloing.

♩=100

C Harmonic Minor Scale

| Fingering: | 2 | 3 | 1 | 3 | 4 | 2 | 3 | 2 | 4 | 3 | 1 | 3 | 2 |

TAB:
```
e|------------------------------------------------------------|
B|------------------------------------------------------------|
G|------------------------2--3--2-----------------------------|
D|--------------1--3--4-----------4--3--1---------------------|
A|--0--2--3------------------------------------3--2-----------|
E|----------------------------------------------------0------|
```

WHOLE TONE SCALE *in C*

The Whole Tone scale creates a dream-like sound becasue each note of the scale is a Whole Tone away (2 frets). The Whole Tone scale was made famous by Impressionist composers such as Claude Debussy and Maurice Ravel. You can also hear this scale in movies and TV shows when the character is dreaming or fantasizing.

Become a **PLATINUM MEMBER** and get access to:

- More Than 20 **Online Courses**.
- Weekly **LIVE Q&As.**
- Monthly **Challenges And Giveaways**.
- Be Part Of The **ULTP NATION**, The Best Ukulele Community.

WHAT THE STUDENTS SAY:

"Great course, taught by a real professional, easy to follow instructions to learning how to solo on your Ukulele.

Great encouragement from Terry Carter throughout the course, helping you to become the soloist and player you want to be.

Kindest regards!"

PETER BAILEY
UKULELE STUDENT.

CREATION
TIME!

Now it's time for you to use all this info and start creating YOUR OWN SOLOS! Yes, you can do it by using the scales you've learned.

Use the blank TABs and the blank Chord Diagrams to write your own pieces. Be creative, be yourself and use your ear to see what chords and notes sound better together.

READY? SET... GO!

TAB

MUSIC SYMBOLS TO KNOW

A variety of symbols, articulations, repeats, hammer on's, pull off's, bends, and slides.

Fermata:
Hold note

Staccato:
Play note short

Accent:
Play note loud

Accented Staccato:
Play note
loud + short

Vibrato
Rapid "shaking"
of note

Arpeggiated Chord:
Play the notes in fast
succession from low
to high strings

Grace Note:
Fast embellishment
note played before
the main note

Mute:
"Muffle" sound of
strings either with
left or right hand

Down Stroke:
Pick string(s) with a
downward motion

Up Stroke:
Pick string(s) with
an upward motion

Tie:
Play first note but
do not play second
note that it is tied to

Ledger Lines:
Extend the staff
higher or lower.

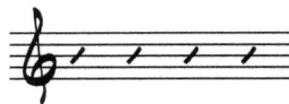

Slash Notation:
Repeat notes & rhythms
from previous measure

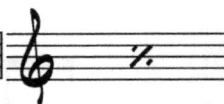

1 Bar Repeat:
Repeat notes &
rhythms from
previous measure

2 Bar Repeat:
Repeat notes & rhythms
from previous 2 measures

Repeat Sign:
(Beginning)

Repeat Sign:
(End)

1st Ending:
Play this part the
first time only

2nd Ending:
Play this part
the second time

(D.C. AL FINE) – *D.C.* (da capo) means go to the beginning of the tune and stop when you get to *Fine*

(D.C. AL CODA) – *D.C.* means go to the beginning of the tune and jump to *Coda* ⊕ when you see the sign ⊕

(D.S. AL FINE) – *D.S.* (dal segno) means go to the *Sign* 𝄋 and stop when you get to *Fine*

(D.S. AL CODA) – *D.S.* means go to the *Sign* 𝄋 And Jump to the *Coda* ⊕ when you see ⊕

SIM... – Play the same rhythm, strum pattern, or picking pattern as the previous measure

ETC... – Continue the same rhythm, strum pattern, or picking pattern as the previous measure

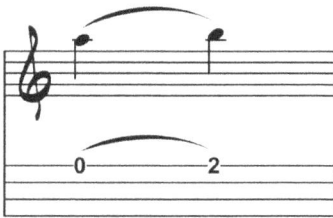

Hammer On:
Pick first note then hammer on to the next note without picking it.

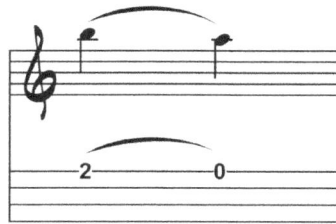

Pull Off:
Pick first note then pull off to the next note without picking it.

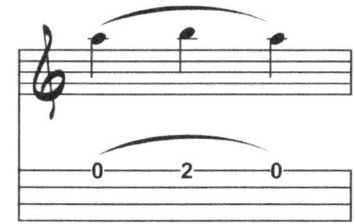

Hammer On & Pull Off:
Pick first note, hammer on to the next note, and pull off to the last note all in one motion.

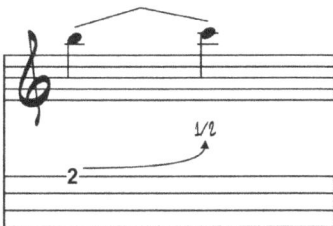

1/2 Step Bend:
Bend the first note a 1/2 step or 1 fret.

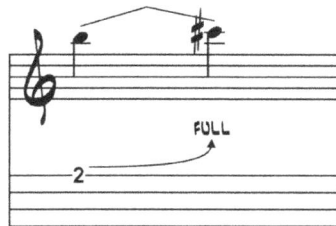

Whole Step Bend:
Bend the first note a whole step or 2 frets.

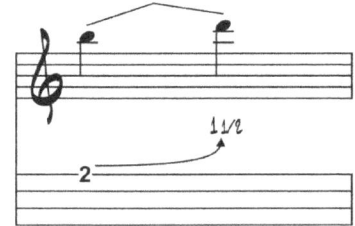

Step & 1/2 Bend:
Bend the first note 1 1/2 steps or 3 frets.

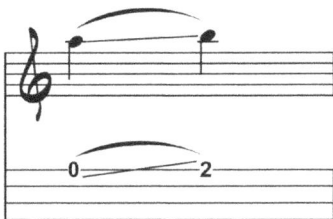

Forward Slide:
Pick first note and slide up to higher note.

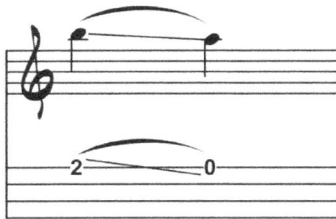

Backward Slide:
Pick first note and slide back to lower note.

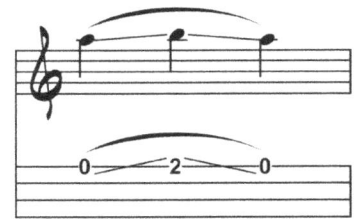

Forward/Backward Slide:
Pick first note, slide up to next note and then slide back.

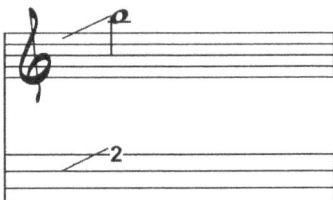

Slide Into Note:
Slide from 2-3 frets below note.

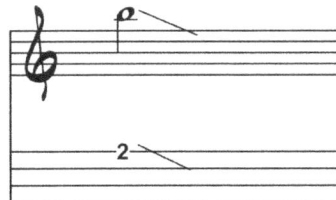

Slide Off Note:
Slide off 2-5 frets after note.

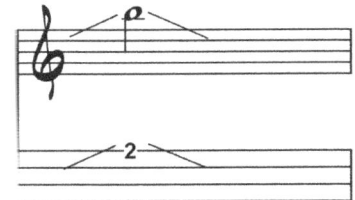

Slide Into Note then Slide Off Note.

38

BASIC RHYTHMS

The 3 main rhythms in this lesson are whole notes, half notes, and quarter notes.

ESSENTIAL RHYTHMS

The 4 rhythms in this lesson are whole notes, half notes, quarter notes and eight notes.

UKULELE PARTS

HEADSTOCK

ULTP SIGNATURE

STRINGS

NUT

FRETS

SIDE DOTS

FRET MARKERS
ON FRETBOARD

SIDE

BODY

FRETBOARD

ROSETTE

SOUND HOLE

TOP

BRIDGE

TUNERS

SADDLE

NECK

BUTT

HEEL

BINDING

SIDE

BACK

TOP 5 TYPE OF WOODS

KOA
THE BEST:
WOODSY AND WARM SOUND
+ LUSH AND POWERFUL

MANGO
THE COOL LOOK:
WARMEST AND MOST POWERFUL
SOUND + WOOD VARIATIONS

ACACIA
THE KOA COUSIN:
BEAUTIFUL LOOK WITH A BOLD,
CLEAR AND WOODSY SOUND

SPRUCE
THE MUSICIAN'S FAVORITE:
POWERFUL PROJECTION,
LOUD AND CLEAR SOUND

MAHOGANY
THE POPULAR:
WOODSY CLEAR SOUND
WITH A GREAT LOOK

UKULELE HANDS

When playing fingerstyle on your ukulele, you will see both letters and numbers to indicate which fingers to use both for picking hand and your fretting hand. These letters and numbers will show up in the music notation, TAB, and/or chord diagrams.

FRETTING HAND	PICKING HAND
The left hand for right-handed players. will be indicated in the music or chord diagrams by numbers:	The right hand for right-handed players. will be indicated in the music by letters:
1=Index finger **3**=Ring finger **2**=Middle finger **4**=Pinky finger	**p**=Thumb **m**=middle **i**=index **a**=ring **c**=pinky (not used in this course)

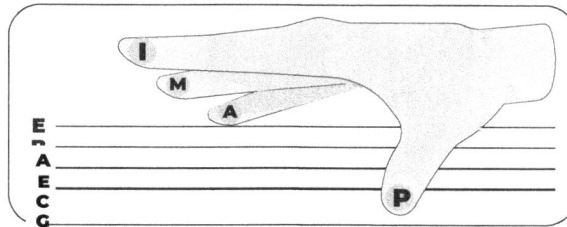

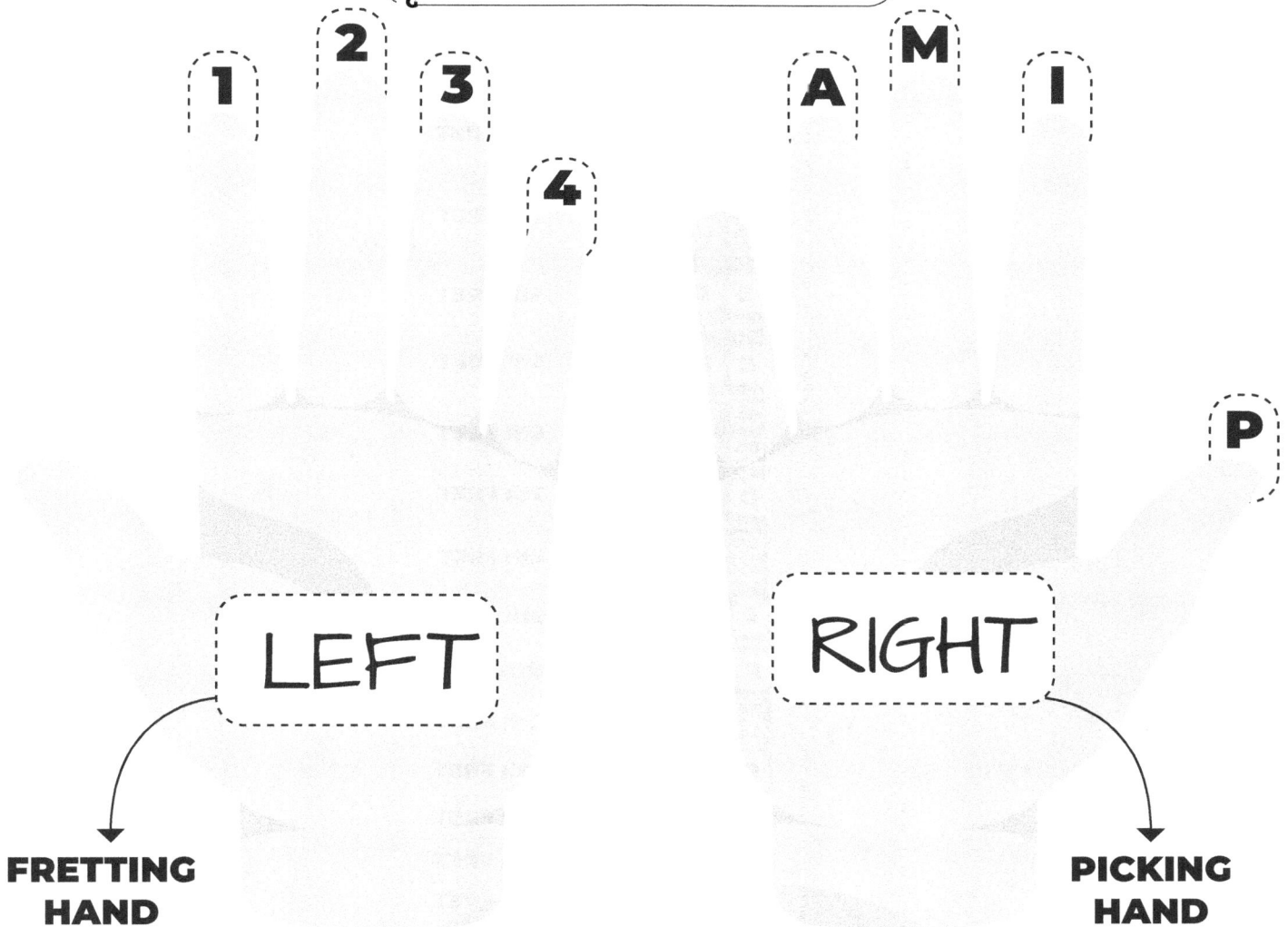

LEFT

FRETTING HAND

RIGHT

PICKING HAND

NOTES ON THE UKULELE NECK

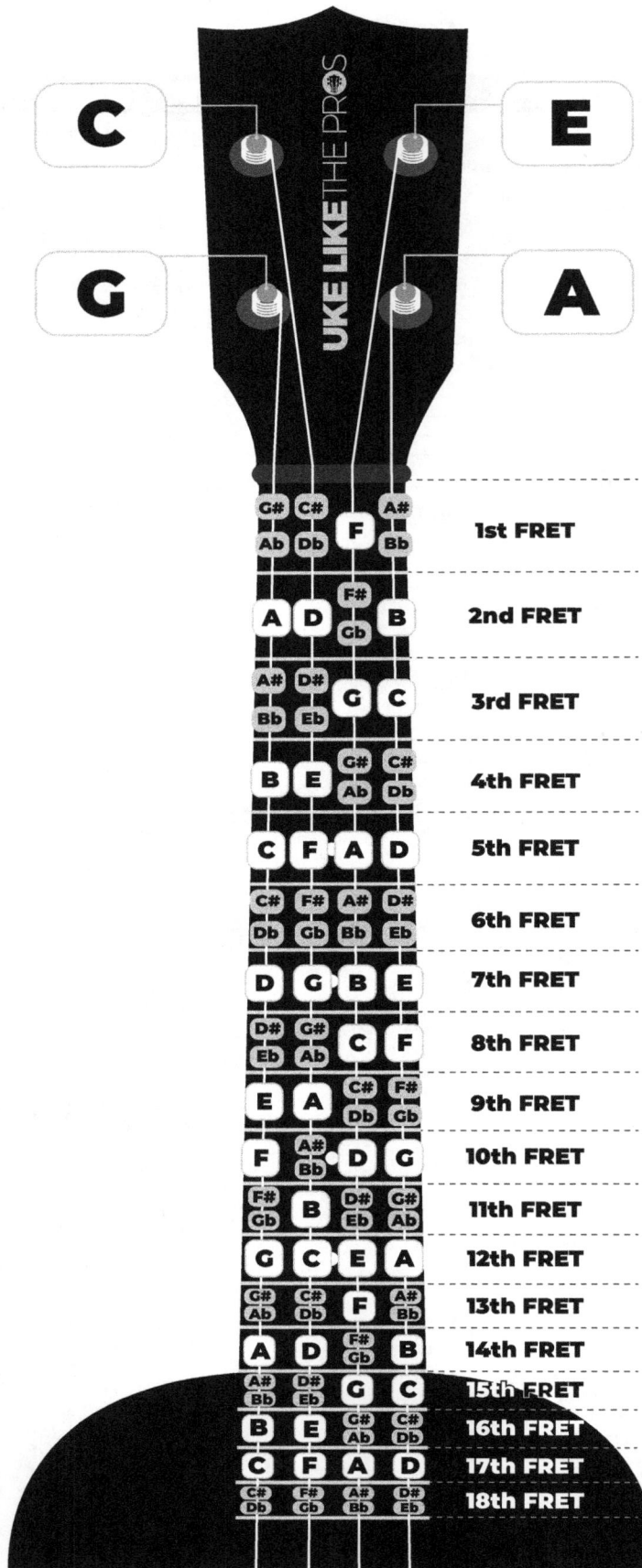

UKE LIKE THE PROS

C			E	
G			A	

String 1	String 2	String 3	String 4	
G#/Ab	C#/Db	F	A#/Bb	**1st FRET**
A	D	F#/Gb	B	**2nd FRET**
A#/Bb	D#/Eb	G	C	**3rd FRET**
B	E	G#/Ab	C#/Db	**4th FRET**
C	F	A	D	**5th FRET**
C#/Db	F#/Gb	A#/Bb	D#/Eb	**6th FRET**
D	G	B	E	**7th FRET**
D#/Eb	G#/Ab	C	F	**8th FRET**
E	A	C#/Db	F#/Gb	**9th FRET**
F	A#/Bb	D	G	**10th FRET**
F#/Gb	B	D#/Eb	G#/Ab	**11th FRET**
G	C	E	A	**12th FRET**
G#/Ab	C#/Db	F	A#/Bb	**13th FRET**
A	D	F#/Gb	B	**14th FRET**
A#/Bb	D#/Eb	G	C	**15th FRET**
B	E	G#/Ab	C#/Db	**16th FRET**
C	F	A	D	**17th FRET**
C#/Db	F#/Gb	A#/Bb	D#/Eb	**18th FRET**

UNDERSTANDING CHORD DIAGRAMS

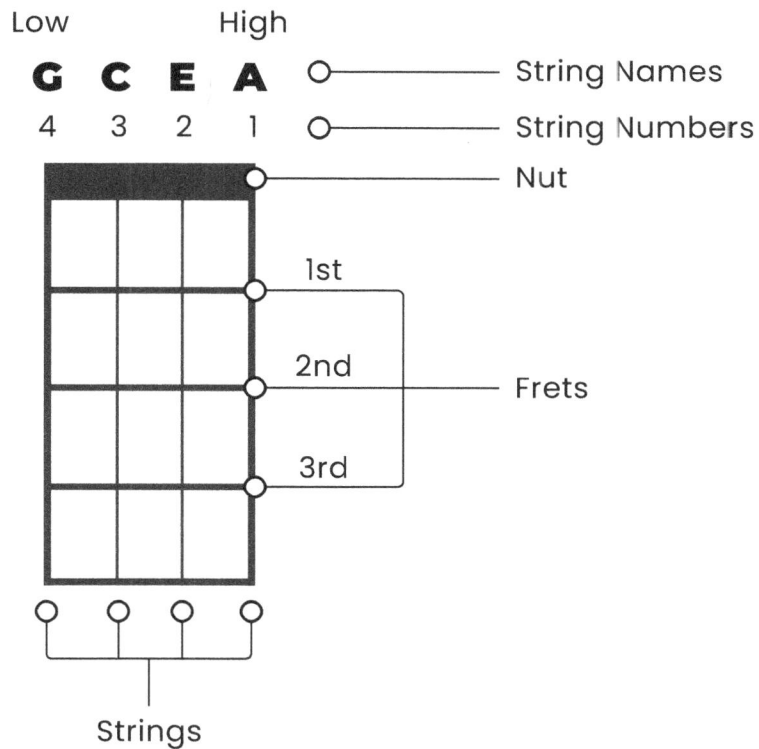

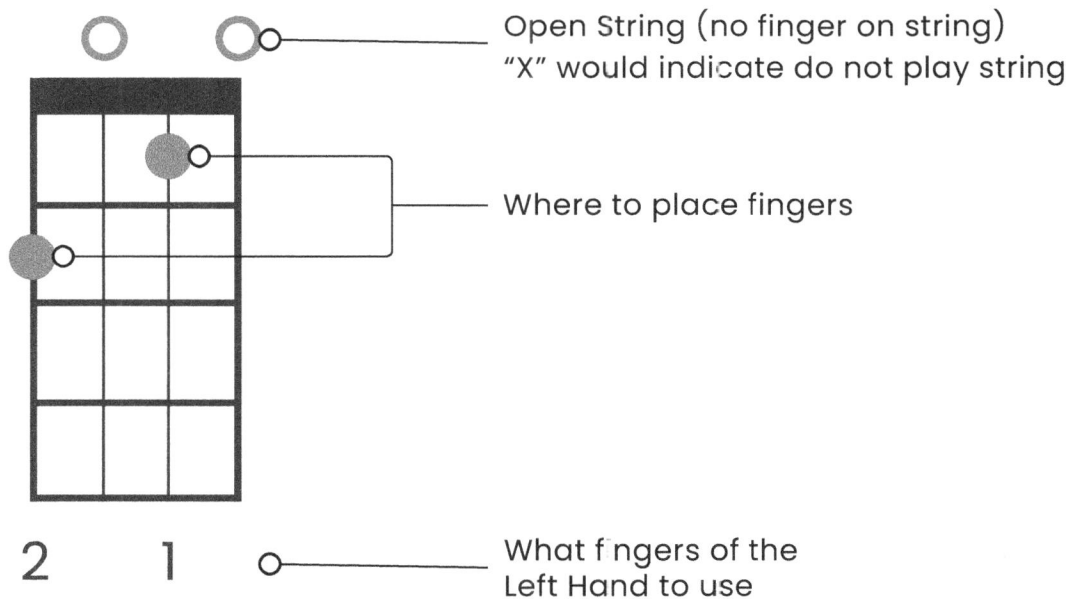

Low   High

G C E A   ⎯ String Names

4   3   2   1   ⎯ String Numbers

⎯ Nut

1st

2nd   ⎯ Frets

3rd

Strings

F   ⎯ Name of Chord

⎯ Open String (no finger on string)
"X" would indicate do not play string

⎯ Where to place fingers

2   1   ⎯ What fingers of the
Left Hand to use

CHORD CHART

These are some of the most widely used chords in all of music. Although there are more chords that are listed, these chords represent the most widely used shapes.

MAJOR CHORDS

A	B	C	D	E	F	G
2 1	3 2 1 1	3	1 1 2	2 2 3 1	2 1	1 3 2

MINOR CHORDS

A min	B min	C min	D min	E min	F min	G min
2	3 1 1 1 (2nd FRET)	3 1 1 1 (3rd FRET)	2 3 1	3 2 1 (2nd FRET)	3 4 2 1 (3rd FRET)	2 3 1

DOMINANT 7th CHORDS

A⁷	B⁷	C⁷	D⁷	E⁷	F⁷	G⁷
1	3 2 1	1	2 3	1 2 3	2 3 1 4	2 1 3

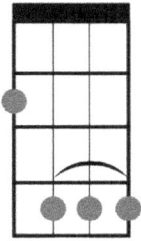 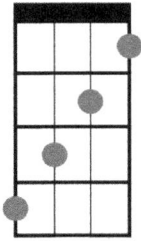 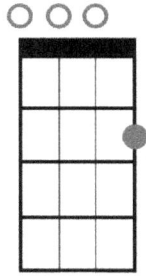 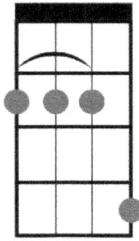 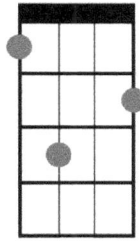 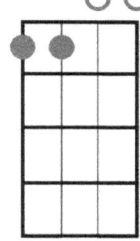 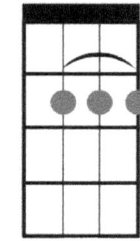

A maj⁷   B maj⁷   C maj⁷   D maj⁷   E maj⁷   F maj⁷   G maj⁷

1 3 3 3   4 3 2 1   2   1 1 1 3   1 3 2   2 3   1 1 1

MINOR 7th CHORDS ──────────────────○

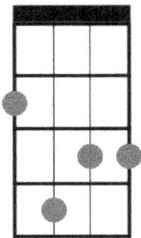 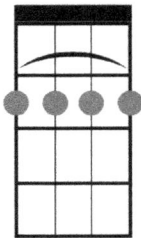 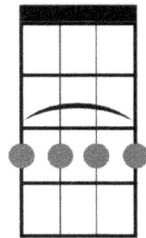 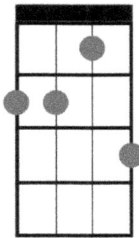 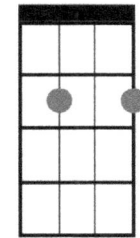 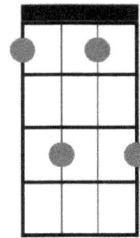 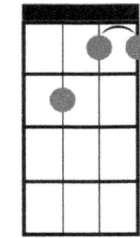

A min⁷   B min⁷   C min⁷   D min⁷   E min⁷   F min⁷   G min⁷

1 4 2 3   1 1 1 1   1 1 1 1   2 3 1 4   2 3   1 3 1 4   2 1 1

SUS + ADD CHORDS ──────────────────○

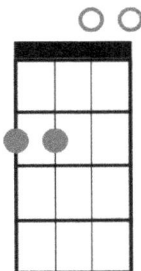 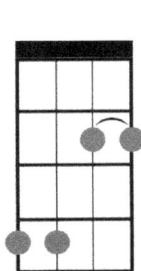 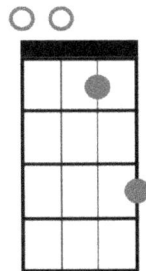 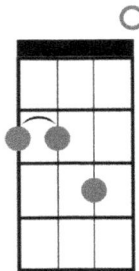 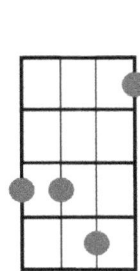 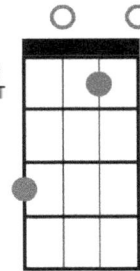 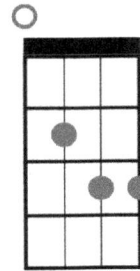

A sus⁴   B sus⁴   C sus⁴   D sus⁴   E sus⁴   F add⁴   G sus⁴

2 3   3 4 1 1   1 3   1 1 3   2 3 4 1   3 1   1 3 4

ABOUT THE AUTHOR

TERRY CARTER

Terry Carter is a San Diego-based business owner, guitar and ukulele player, surfer, songwriter, and creator of the #1 music sites *rocklikethepros.com, ukelikethepros.com* and *terrycartermusicstore.com*. With over 25 years as a professional musician, educator, and Los Angeles studio musician, Terry has worked with greats like Weezer, Josh Groban, Robby Krieger (The Doors), 2-time Grammy-winning composer Christopher Tin (Calling All Dawns), Duff McKagan (Guns N' Roses), Grammy-winning producer Charles Goodan (Santana/Rolling Stones), and the Los Angeles Philharmonic.

Terry has written and produced tracks for commercials (Discount Tire and Puma) and TV shows, including Scorpion (CBS), Pit Bulls & Parolees (Animal Planet), Trippin', Wildboyz, and The Real World (MTV). He has self-published over 10 books for Uke Like The Pros and Rock Like The Pros, filmed over 30 ukulele and guitar online courses, and has over 140,000 subscribers on his Uke Like The Pros YouTube channel.

Terry received a Master of Music in Studio/Jazz Guitar Performance from University of Southern California and a Bachelor of Music from San Diego State University, with an emphasis in Jazz Studies and Music Education. He has taught at the University of Southern California, San Diego State University, Santa Monica College, Miracosta College, and Los Angeles Trade Tech College.

Find out more about Terry Carter at: terrycarter.com

TERRY CARTER

ALL YOUR MUSIC NEEDS AT:
TERRYCARTERMUSICSTORE.COM

Ukuleles

Guitars

Cases

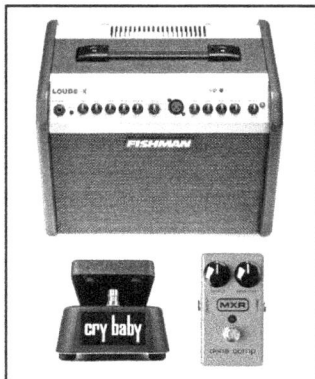
Amplifiers and Pedals

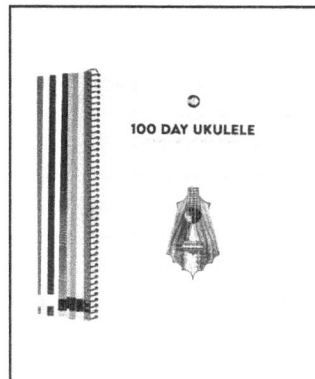
Books

Accessories

ONLINE UKULELE COURSES

The perfect place to learn how to play Ukulele, Guitar, Baritone or Guitarlele.

ULTP Roadmap
WHERE TO START?

1) UKULELE BEGINNER
A. Beginning Ukulele Starter Course
B. Beginning Ukulele Bootcamp Course
C. Ukulele Fundamentals Course
D. Ukulele Practice & Technique Course
E. Master the Ukulele 1

2) UKULELE INTERMEDIATE
A. Master The Ukulele 2
B. Beginning Music Reading
C. 23 Ultimate Chord Progressions
D. Beginning Ukulele Fingerstyle Course

3) UKULELE ADVANCED
A. Ukulele Blues Mastery Course
B. Beginning Ukulele Soloing Course
C. Fingerstyle Mastery Course
D. Jazz Swing Mastery Course

MORE OPTIONS!

FUNLAND
A. Beginning Ukulele Kids Course Songbook
B. 21 Popular Songs for Ukulele
C. The Best Ukulele Christmas Songs
D. 10 Classic Rock Licks
E. Guitar Fundamentals

BARITONE UKULELE
A. Beginning Baritone Ukulele Bootcamp Course
B. 6 Weeks Baritone Q&A
C. Baritone Blues Mastery Course
D. Beginning Baritone Fingerstyle Course

GUITARLELE
A. Guitarlele Starter Course
B. 6 Weeks Guitarlele Q&A
C. Guitarlele Course for Ukulele and Guitar Players
D. Guitarlele Blues Mastery Course

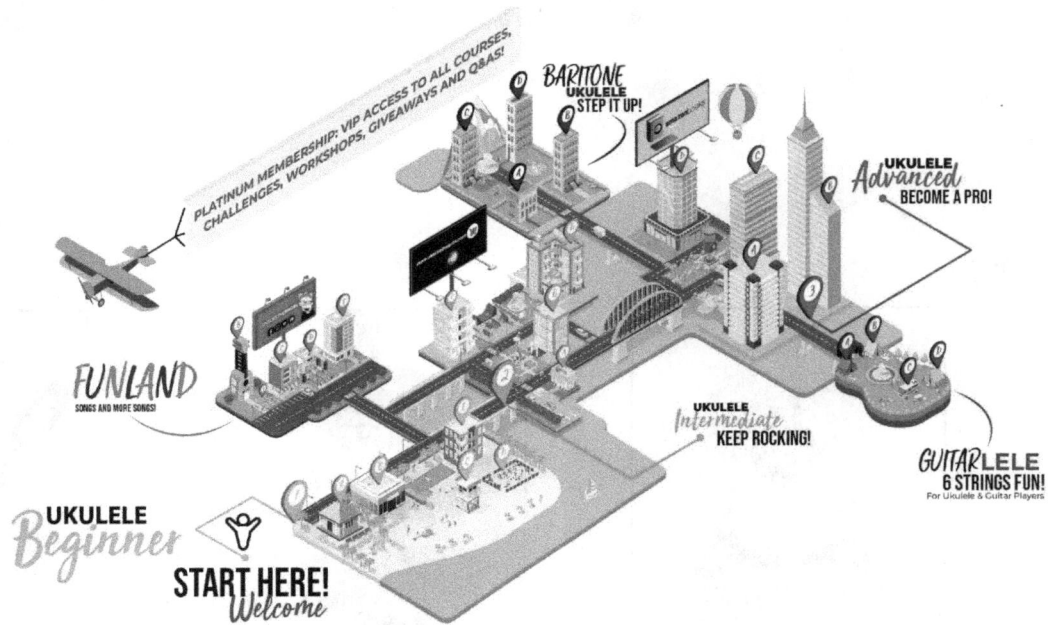

Courses For All Levels

UKELIKETHEPROS.COM

UKELIKETHEPROS.COM
BLOG.UKELIKETHEPROS.COM
TERRYCARTERMUSICSTORE.COM

@ukelikethepros